BLACK TRAILBLAZERS IN SPORTS

ARTHUR ASHE

by David Lee Morgan Jr.

FOCUS READERS

NAVIGATOR

WWW.FOCUSREADERS.COM

Focus Readers is distributed by North Star Editions:
sales@northstareditions.com | 888-417-0195

Produced for Focus Readers by Red Line Editorial.

Photographs ©: AP Images, cover, 1, 4–5; Bettmann/Getty Images, 6, 21, 25; UPI/Bettmann Archive/Bettmann/Getty Images, 9; Richmond Times-Dispatch/AP Images, 10–11; Afro American Newspapers/Gado/Archive Photos/Getty Images, 13; Harry Harris/AP Images, 15; Edward A. Hausner/New York Times Co./Archive Photos/Getty Images, 16–17; PhotoQuest/Archive Photos/Getty Images, 19; Robert Dear/AP Images, 22–23; Nik Kleinberg/The Chronicle Collection/Getty Images, 27; Red Line Editorial, 29

Library of Congress Cataloging-in-Publication Data
Names: Morgan, David Lee, author.
Title: Arthur Ashe / by David Lee Morgan Jr.
Description: Mendota Heights, MN: Focus Readers, [2025] | Series: Black trailblazers in sports | Includes bibliographical references and index. | Audience: Grades 4-6
Identifiers: LCCN 2024001386 (print) | LCCN 2024001387 (ebook) | ISBN 9798889982081 (hardcover) | ISBN 9798889982647 (paperback) | ISBN 9798889983712 (pdf) | ISBN 9798889983200 (ebook)
Subjects: LCSH: Ashe, Arthur | Tennis players--United States--Biography--Juvenile literature. | African American tennis players--Biography--Juvenile literature.
Classification: LCC GV994.A7 M66 2025 (print) | LCC GV994.A7 (ebook) | DDC 796.342092 [B]--dc23/eng/20240118
LC record available at https://lccn.loc.gov/2024001386
LC ebook record available at https://lccn.loc.gov/2024001387

Printed in the United States of America
Mankato, MN
082024

ABOUT THE AUTHOR

David Lee Morgan Jr. is the author of 11 books, including *LeBron James: The Rise of a Star* and *Breaking Through the Lines: The Marion Motley Story*. Morgan was a longtime sportswriter with the *Akron Beacon Journal* and is now a high school English teacher and public speaker.

TABLE OF CONTENTS

VIOUS SETS
S.CONNORS
A.R.ASHE
2 3

CHAPTER 1

WINNING AT WIMBLEDON

Arthur Ashe stepped onto the court. He was playing in the 1975 Wimbledon men's singles final. Ashe was a Black man who was nearly 32 years old. He faced Jimmy Connors, a white man who was only 22. Connors was ranked No. 1 in the world. He was also the defending Wimbledon champion.

Arthur Ashe hits a backhand return to Jimmy Connors in the 1975 Wimbledon Final.

Ashe stretches for the ball during the 1975 Wimbledon Final.

Connors was full of confidence. Some people called him cocky. He had not lost one set on his way to the final. Plus, Ashe was much older than Connors. So, most people thought Connors would win easily.

Ashe studied the way Connors played. Powerful shots didn't work against him. Connors simply hit the ball back even harder. Ashe usually depended on his power to win matches. But he knew he had to try something different.

So, Ashe kept Connors off balance. He let Connors attack. Then Ashe returned the ball with slow shots. He used lots of spin. He also used every inch of the court. That kept Connors running from side to side. Then Ashe used drop shots. Those shots made Connors run quickly from the back of the court to the net.

Ashe's strategy worked. He used brains instead of brawn. He used his wisdom and experience. Ashe crushed Connors in the first two sets, 6–1, 6–1. Then Connors adjusted. He won the third set 7–5. In the fourth set, Ashe began hitting powerful shots. The change threw Connors off. Ashe took the set 6–4 to win the match.

CONNORS VS. ASHE

The 1975 Wimbledon final was the only time Arthur Ashe beat Jimmy Connors. Before the match, they had played each other three times. Connors won all three matches. In his career, Connors was 6–1 against Ashe. But Ashe's one win was the match most people remember.

Ashe raises his trophy after winning the 1975 Wimbledon men's singles championship.

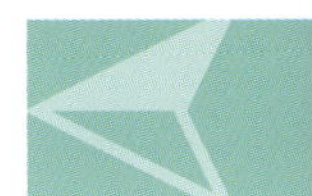

Tennis experts considered it one of the biggest upsets in the sport's history. Ashe also made history. He became the first Black man ever to win Wimbledon.

SMALL LOAN CORP
491
25 SKIDOO
1888
GOODBYE RICHMOND!
1949

CHAPTER 2

WHERE IT ALL STARTED

Arthur Ashe was born on July 10, 1943, in Richmond, Virginia. His parents were Arthur Ashe Sr. and Mattie Ashe. Arthur had a younger brother, Johnnie.

Mattie taught her sons to follow the rules, work hard in school, and be polite. However, she died just before Arthur turned seven. After that, Arthur and his

In the 1940s, nearly 200,000 people lived in Richmond, Virginia. Approximately one-third were Black.

brother were raised by their father. Arthur Sr. wanted to make sure his kids stayed in line and followed their mother's rules. So, he took them to church every Sunday.

Arthur grew up under Jim Crow. This was a system of **racist** laws. Some laws **segregated** areas based on race. So, Arthur couldn't play on public tennis courts. They were for white people only.

Even so, Arthur found a way to play. His family's house was in the middle of Brook Field. This was a Black-only park. Arthur's father worked at the park. Arthur started learning to play tennis there.

Arthur's first coach was Ronald Charity. He was one of the best Black tennis

Racial segregation of public areas was common under Jim Crow.

players in the United States. Charity helped Arthur improve his game. Arthur won a national youth title at 10 years old.

Charity introduced Arthur to Dr. Walter Johnson. Johnson coached Althea Gibson.

She later became the first Black person to win three of the four **Grand Slam** titles. Under Johnson, Arthur continued to improve. He became a top-ranked junior player.

At home, Arthur struggled to find good competition. Segregation limited the players he could face. In response, he traveled during the summers. Then, for his last year of high school, he went to St. Louis, Missouri. He met better players there.

Arthur excelled in both tennis and school. He finished high school as the top student in his class. By then, his tennis talent was known across the country. In

A 16-year-old Arthur Ashe (far right) shakes hands with opponents before a doubles match in 1959.

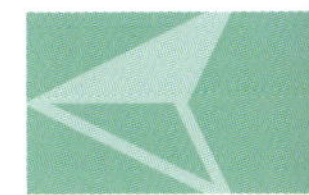

1960, the magazine *Sports Illustrated* printed a story on him. Arthur also received a **scholarship** to the University of California, Los Angeles (UCLA).

Wilson

CHAPTER 3

THE RISE TO THE TOP

Arthur Ashe began attending UCLA in 1961. At the time, UCLA had one of the best college tennis programs in the country. Ashe quickly became a top player on the team. He was so good that he made history in 1963. He was selected to play in the Davis Cup. In the Davis Cup, countries compete against one another.

Ashe gets ready to compete at the 1963 US Open.

Ashe was the first Black player on the US team.

In 1965, Ashe dominated at the college level. He won the National Collegiate Athletic Association (NCAA) singles title. He won the doubles title, too. His

A BROTHER'S SACRIFICE

Arthur's brother, Johnnie, served in the US military. He joined at age 17 in 1965. Johnnie fought in the Vietnam War (1955–75). His first tour ended in 1968. He could have left the military then. But he knew the military usually didn't send siblings at the same time. And Johnnie didn't want Arthur to have to fight. So, Johnnie served a second tour. Johnnie's choice helped Arthur's tennis career take off.

In 1965, Ashe led UCLA to an undefeated 11–0 season.

success helped UCLA win the NCAA championship that year.

Ashe graduated from UCLA in 1966. After that, he entered the US Army. He served for two years. But he did not have to fight overseas. During this time, he continued to play tennis.

In 1968, Ashe broke onto the world stage. He reached the final in the US Open. There, he faced Tom Okker. Ashe relied on the strongest parts of his game. He used quick wrist action to strike powerful backhands. He placed his shots carefully, too. Ashe also smashed his serves. He recorded 26 aces. An ace is when the other player does not even touch the serve. Ashe attacked with a **serve and volley** as well.

Ashe beat Okker in five sets. He'd just won his first Grand Slam. Ashe was the first Black man ever to win the US Open. He soon rose to the No. 1 rank in the United States.

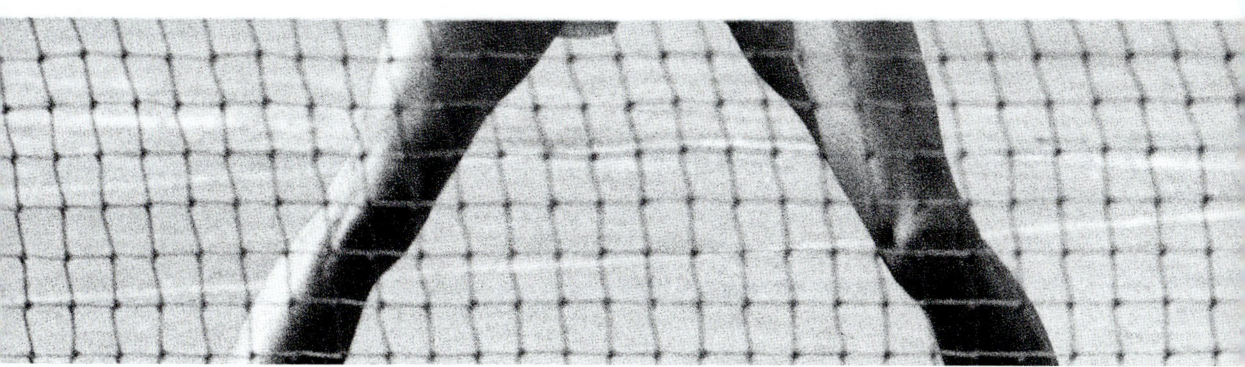

Ashe was 25 years old when he won the 1968 US Open.

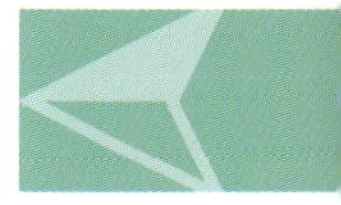

CHAPTER 4

STANDING UP FOR WHAT'S RIGHT

In 1969, Arthur Ashe tried to play in the South African Open. But South Africa had a racist policy called **apartheid**. The white government oppressed its Black population. South Africa denied Ashe's **visa** request. Ashe couldn't travel there.

Ashe notched his second Grand Slam in 1970. He won the Australian Open.

Ashe competes in a match at Wimbledon in 1970.

He had become one of the world's most famous tennis players. But Ashe still couldn't get into South Africa. He applied for a visa in 1970. But he was rejected again. In response, Ashe spoke out against apartheid. He helped get South Africa kicked out of the Davis Cup.

YANNICK NOAH

In 1971, Ashe met 11-year-old Yannick Noah in Cameroon, West Africa. Ashe thought the boy had great talent for tennis. So, Ashe helped him go to France to train. In 1983, Noah won the French Open. He became the first Black man to do so. As of 2023, Ashe and Noah were still the only Black men to win Grand Slams.

Ashe sits as a witness in 1970 to testify against apartheid in South Africa.

South Africa denied Ashe's visa for two more years. Then, in 1973, the country changed course. Ashe finally competed in the South African Open. While he was there, he saw how poorly Black people were treated.

In 1975, Ashe reached the height of his tennis career. He won Wimbledon. That earned him the No. 2 ranking in the world.

Ashe's career came to a sudden end in 1979. He suffered a heart attack. He was just 36 years old. As a result, he retired in 1980. Even so, Ashe remained committed to justice. He kept protesting against South African apartheid.

In 1988, Ashe learned he had HIV. This virus can lead to a disease called AIDS. At the time, many people attached **stigma** to this illness. Ashe became an activist for HIV and AIDS.

Ashe (center) marches with legendary activist Harry Belafonte (right) against South African apartheid in 1985.

Ashe died from an AIDS-related illness in 1993. He was 49 years old. People remembered Ashe for his amazing tennis talents. They also remembered him for his powerful work for justice.

ARTHUR ASHE

- **Height:** 6 feet 1 inch (185 cm)
- **Weight:** 160 pounds (73 kg)
- **Born:** July 10, 1943
- **Died:** February 6, 1993
- **Birthplace:** Richmond, Virginia
- **High school:** Maggie L. Walker (Richmond, Virginia) (1957–60); Charles Sumner (St. Louis, Missouri) (1960–61)
- **College:** University of California, Los Angeles (1961–66)
- **Major achievements:** NCAA champion (1965); US Open Singles Champion (1968); Australian Open Singles Champion (1970); French Open Doubles Champion (1971); Wimbledon Singles Champion (1975); Australian Open Doubles Champion (1977); International Tennis Hall of Fame (1985); Presidential Medal of Freedom (1993)

New York
(US Open)
St. Louis
Richmond
Los Angeles
London
(Wimbledon)
Paris
(French Open)
Sydney
(Australian Open)
Johannesburg
(South African Open)

FOCUS ON
ARTHUR ASHE

Write your answers on a separate piece of paper.

1. Write a paragraph explaining the main ideas of Chapter 4.
2. How do you think athletes should use their fame for the issues they care about? Why?
3. Which Grand Slam did Arthur Ashe win first?
   - **A.** Australian Open
   - **B.** Wimbledon
   - **C.** US Open
4. What is one way Ashe helped future generations of Black tennis players?
   - **A.** Ashe kept playing even after his heart attack.
   - **B.** Ashe never tried to play in South Africa.
   - **C.** Ashe met and helped Yannick Noah.

Answer key on page 32.

GLOSSARY

apartheid

A system of racial segregation in South Africa from the late 1940s until the early 1990s.

Grand Slam

One of the four major tennis events. They include the Australian Open, the French Open, Wimbledon, and the US Open.

racist

Having to do with hatred or mistreatment of people because of their skin color or ethnicity.

scholarship

Money given to a student to pay for education expenses.

segregated

Separated or set apart based on race, gender, or religion.

serve and volley

When a tennis player runs to the net right after serving in order to hit the return in midair.

stigma

Unfair and harmful ideas that a large group of people have about something.

visa

A type of legal permission to be in a country.

TO LEARN MORE

BOOKS

Dodson, Judy Allen. *The Ashe Brothers: How Arthur and Johnnie Changed Tennis Forever.* North Mankato, MN: Capstone Editions, 2023.

Fishman, Jon M. *Tennis's G.O.A.T.: Serena Williams, Roger Federer, and More*. Minneapolis: Lerner Publications, 2022.

Nash, Sibylla. *Athletes for Racial Equity: Jackie Robinson, Arthur Ashe, and More*. North Mankato, MN: Capstone Press, 2022.

NOTE TO EDUCATORS

Visit **www.focusreaders.com** to find lesson plans, activities, links, and other resources related to this title.

INDEX

Answer Key: 1. Answers will vary; **2.** Answers will vary; **3.** C; **4.** C